Honey Served
On Thorns

Honey Served On Thorns

A COMMEMORATIVE CHAPBOOK
For LOLA RIDGE
on the 150th anniversary of her birth

Gabriel Rosenstock

An chéad chló © 2023 Gabriel Rosenstock

ISBN: 978-1-7395610-2-4

Foilsithe ag Poets of the Planet, 26 Rue Delambre, 75014 Paris, France.

Ealaín an chlúdaigh: New York Street at Dusk (1908)
Louis Michel Eilshemius (1864-1941) ©Artvee

Dearadh: Daire Ó Beaglaoich, Graftrónaic

"Lola Ridge is an exemplary case of an overlooked Irish woman poet of major talent, whose life and career failed to follow a conventional path, and who is only now receiving her full critical due." *

---

* Tobin, D. (2021). Accidental Irishness and the Transnational Legacy of Lola Ridge. In A. Darcy & D. Wheatley (Eds.), A History of Irish Women's Poetry (pp. 223-238). Cambridge: Cambridge University Press. doi:10.1017/9781108778596.014

The poems selected here are in Public Domain. Gabriel Rosenstock's Irish-language transcreations are issued as Open Content under a Creative Commons Attribution 4.0 International (CC-BY 4.0). This means that the Irish-language versions may be used by anyone without seeking permission and may be adapted, performed, republished and reproduced in any creative form whatsoever. The same goes for John McDonald's fine transcreations in Scots.

Why Scots? It's a little nod to her Glasgow-born partner, David Lawson, an Anarchist through whom she got to know such others in the field as Alexander Berkman: no fiercer critic of British policy in Ireland could you find! (Scots, by the way, is a language often ignored when we speak of a multilingual world).

Irish-born Lola Ridge arrived in New York in 1908 via New Zealand and Australia which were both voluntary and involuntary destinations for many Irish and Scots, and her subsequent travels took her to many parts of America, a melting pot for hundreds of cultures. She anticipated the global, multicultural societies we find in so many parts of the world today. In the 1930s she would travel to Paris, Beirut, Baghdad, Taos and Mexico.

The anti-copyright status of the Scots and Irish-language versions in this commemorative chapbook would surely have pleased the Anarchist in Lola Ridge. We are quite sure that she would warmly approve of these Irish-language transcreations of seven of her poems (and more in the Afterword) as she could trace her ancestors back to pre-Conquest Gaelic Ireland.

Two of her poems here are directly concerned with Irish history, her poem to Big Jim Larkin, labour leader, and the 1916 poem in which she regrets not having had a chance to fight in the GPO with Connolly, Pearse and the others. When we think of the feistiness of those days, in Ireland and in the US, what happened? Have they put something in the water?!

∼

An Fidléir appeared in *Poetry Ireland Review*, Issue 140, 2023.

∼

The publishers gratefully acknowledge Masood Hussain, Kashmir, for his insightful portrait of Lola Ridge. Masood and Gabriel have collaborated on many projects together, including *Walk with Gandhi* (2019) which is available as a free digital edition for Young Adults from Free Kids Books; *Boatman! take these songs from me* (Manipal Universal Press, India, 2023) and *Love Letter to Kashmir* (Cross-Cultural Communications, New York, 2023).

∼

The publishers gratefully acknowledge The Eblana Club, Dún Laoghaire, Ireland, for their assistance.

This commemorative chapbook is published in association with POP (Poets of the Planet) 26 Rue Delambre, 75014 Paris, France. It is the first title from POP.

Who fears to think of Lola Ridge? Those who have not heard of her. This is poetry that spits in your face with a savage beauty, that speaks to the world in her own time and in ours.

 Cé eile ach Gabriel Rosenstock a chuirfeadh Gaeilge uirthi? File í a fhreagraíonn go hiomlán dá mheon féin, meon sin na saoirse gan teorainn, meon na spride ar chosa in airde, meon nach bhfónann ceangal. Dícheall aon duine fíoch agus filíocht a nascadh le chéile, ach tá déanta anseo le binneas cruinn.

– Alan Titley

∼

Lola Ridge is an exemplar of the Outsider Poet. Long before her time, and dead long before ours, her poetry seeps into our reading minds from its own uncompromising, liminal place. Reading her now is to cross a threshold not to the past, but to an imminent prophecy of the present, one that threatens to arrive before we do. Hers is the voice we hear on waking, intoning its songs replete with metaphor, telling us to get up, to straighten ourselves, to be part of the Moment that we are in danger of wasting.

– John W. Sexton

∼

A taster volume to whet the appetite for the poems, life, and times, of Lola Ridge. The trilingual presentation highlights the supranational relevance of her work, and an afterword by Gabriel Rosenstock positions Ridge as an empathetic and socially engaged writer whose themes have a strikingly contemporary resonance. Honey Served on Thorns is a welcome addition to the growing literature about this luminous poet.

– Amanda Bell

∼

Lola Ridge's work combines Imagist observation with an uninhibited passion for justice. Her finest poems prove that emotion is what invigorates art, not flamboyant wordplay. Rage and tenderness are companions here. Her life awaits reinterpretation by a novelist of stature.

– Rory Brennan

Clár/Contents

Palestine 1
An Phalaistín 2
Palestine 3
The Fiddler 4
An Fidléir 5
The Fiddler 6
To Larkin 7
Don Lorcánach 8
To Larkin 9
The Fire 10
An Tine 11
The Lowe 12
Wall Street at Night 13
Wall Street Istoíche 14
Wall Street It Nicht 15
Mother 16
Máthair 17
Mither 18
The Tidings (Easter 1916) 19
Scéala ó Éirinn (1916) 20
The Tidings (Easter 1916) 21
Iarfhocal/Afterword 22
A Chríoch/End 32

A portrait by Masood Hussain of Lola Ridge, born 12 December 1873, Dolphin's Barn, Dublin, died 19 May, 1941, Brooklyn, NY.

Palestine

Old plant of Asia—
Mutilated vine
Holding earth's leaping sap
In every stem and shoot
That lopped off, sprouts again—
Why should you seek a plateau walled about,
Whose garden is the world?

An Phalaistín

Planda ársa na hÁise—
Fíniún scriosta
Sú an domhain ag éirí
I ngach gas díot, i ngach péac
A fhásann arís i ndiaidh a scoite—
Cén fáth a mbeadh ardchlár múrtha uaitse,
Nuair is é an domhan do gharraíse?

Palestine

Auld plantie o Asia—
Tasht vine
Hauden yirth's lowpin sap
In ilk shank and spirl
Thit sned, sproots aince mair—
Whit wey suid ye reenge fir a plateau wallit aboot,
Whaes gairden's the hail warl?

The Fiddler

In a little Hungarian café
Men and women are drinking
Yellow wine in tall goblets.

Through the milky haze of the smoke,
The fiddler, undersized, blond,
Leans to his violin
As to the breast of a woman.
Red hair kindles to fire
On the black of his coat-sleeve,
Where his white thin hand
Trembles and dives,
Like a sliver of moonlight,
When wind has broken the water.

An Fidléir

I gcaife beag Ungárach
Tá fíon buí á ól as cuacha arda
Ag fir is mná.

Trí smúiteán modartha an deataigh,
Claonann an fidléir beag fionn
I dtreo a veidhlín
Faoi mar ba bhrollach mná é.
A ghruaig rua ina lasair
I nduibhe mhuinchille a chóta,
Tumann a lámh thanaí chailce
Is í ar crith mar shliseog
De sholas na gealaí
Nuair a bhriseann an ghaoth an t-uisce.

The Fiddler

In a peerie Hungarian café
Fowk'r sowpin yalla wine
Frae lang tassies.

Throuch a mulky loom o reek,
The fiddler, shilpit, fair heidit,
Healds tae's fiddle
As tae a wumman's breist.
Reid herr kennles tae lowe
On the bleck o's cot-sleeve,
Whaur his pirlie fite haun
trummles an dooks
Lik a skelf o muinlicht
Whan wund's brucken the watter.

To Larkin

Is it you I see go by the window, Jim Larkin—
you not looking at me nor any one,
And your shadow swaying from East to West?
Strange that you should be walking free—
you shut down without light,
And your legs tied up with a knot of iron
One hundred million men and women go inevitably
about their affairs,
In the somnolent way

Of men before a great drunkenness…
They do not see you go by their windows, Jim Larkin,
With your eyes bloody as the sunset
And your shadow gaunt upon the sky…
You, and the like of you, that life
Is crushing for their frantic wines.

Don Lorcánach

An tusa a fheicimse ag dul thar an bhfuinneog, a Lorcánaigh—
is nílir ag breathnú ormsa ná ar éinne,
Is do scáil ag luascadh Soir is Siar?
Is ait liom cead do chos a bheith agat—
is tú faoi ghlas gan solas,
Snaidhm iarainn ar do chosa.

Fir is mná gan áireamh i mbun a ngnó mar is gnách,
Suansiúl an tslua
Roimis na meisce móire…
Ní fheiceann siad ag gabháil thar a bhfuinneoga thú, a Lorcánaigh,
Is do shúile chomh fuilteach le luí na gréine
Do scáil lom in aghaidh na spéire…
Tú féin is do leithéidse is an saol do d'fháscadh
Ar mhaithe lena bhfíonta buile.

To Larkin

Is't yersel ah glisk gaun by the winnock, Jim Larkin—
Naither goavin it me nor onieyin,
An yer sheddae sweyin frae East tae Wast?
Unco thit ye suid be stravaigin lowse—
You steekit doon athoot licht,

An yer legs
Shackelt in a kinch o airn.
A hunner million fowk gae aboot thair troke,
In the sleeperie wey
O chiels afore a muckle drouthiness…
They dinnae glisk ye gaun by thair winnocks, Jim Larkin,
Wi yer een bluidy as the sinset
An yer sheddae peesweep i the lift…
You an the lik o you, thit life
Is broozlin fir thair dancin-mad wines.

The Fire

The old men of the world have made a fire
To warm their trembling hands.
They poke the young men in.
The young men burn like withes.

If one run a little way,
The old men are wrath.
They catch him and bind him and throw him again to the flames.

Green withes burn slow…
And the smoke of the young men's torment
Rises round and sheer as the trunk of a pillared oak,
And the darkness thereof spreads over the sky…
Green withes burn slow…

And the old men of the world sit round the fire
And rub their hands…
But the smoke of the young men's torment
Ascends up for ever and ever.

An Tine

Tá tine lasta ag seanóirí an domhain
Chun a lámha creathacha a ghoradh.
Cothaíd an tine sin le slatairí óga.
Na fir óga á ndó acu mar a dhófaí gad.

Má éalaíonn macaomh uathu
Beidh goimh ar na seanóirí.
Béarfaidh siad air, ceanglófar é, caithfear chun na lasracha

Arís é. Dónn gad glas go mall…
Agus an ghal ó chéasadh na bhfear óg
Ag éirí go cruinn, chomh hard le tamhan colúnach darach,
An doircheacht ag leathnú ar fud na spéire…

Is mall a dhónn an gad glas…
Agus suíonn seanóirí an domhain seo timpeall na tine
A lámha á gcuimilt acu…
Gal na bhfear óg céasta, áfach,
Éiríonn in airde gan stad gan staonadh.

The Lowe

The bodachs o the warl hae wrocht a lowe
Tae beek thair trummlin hauns.
They prog the youthlins in.
The youthlins brenn lik sauchs.

Gin yin rins aff,
The bodachs are wraith.
They nick'm, yerk'm, an fling'm intae the lowe agane.

Emerant sauchs brenn slawly…
An the reek o the youthlin's deave
Heizes roond an evendoon as the caber o an aik,
An the derkness frae't spreids ower the lift…

Emerant sauchs brenn slaw…
An the bodachs o the warl hunker roon the lowe
An dicht thair hauns…
Bit the reek o the youthlin's deave
Heizes up fir aye!

Wall Street at Night

Long vast shapes
Cooled and flushed through with darkness.
Lidless windows
Glazed with a flashy lustre
From some little pert café chirping up like a sparrow.
And down among iron guts
Piled silver
Throwing grey spatter of light… pale without heat…
Like the pallor of dead bodies.

Wall Street Istoíche

Cruthanna fada fairsinge
Fuaraithe agus sruthlaithe le dorchadas.
Fuinneoga ag stánadh orainn
Glónraithe le loinnir phreabach
Ó chaife beag dána atá ag giolcadh mar ghealbhan.
Agus thíos i measc an ionathair iarainn
Airgead ina charn
Sprais liath uaidh… mílítheach gan teas…
Ar nós báine corpán.

Wall Street It Nicht

Lang muckle shapes
Cuilt an reenged wi derkness.
Lidless winnocks
Lozenit wi a fantoosh glowe
Frae sum peerie cafe cheeplin up lik a speuggie.
An doon amang airn puddins
Stackit siller
Skailin gray splairge o licht… whitely athoot waarmth…
Lik the huil o the deid

Mother

Your love was like moonlight
turning harsh things to beauty,
so that little wry souls
reflecting each other obliquely
as in cracked mirrors…
beheld in your luminous spirit
their own reflection,
transfigured as in a shining stream,
and loved you for what they are not.
You are less an image in my mind
than a lustre
I see you in gleams
pale as star-light on a grey wall…
evanescent as the reflection of a white swan
shimmering in broken water.

Máthair

Mar sholas na gealaí a bhí do ghrása
nithe garbha á n-iompú ina n-áilleacht
i dtreo is go raibh anamacha searbha
i bhfrithchaitheamh fiar a chéile
mar a bheadh i scátháin scoilte…
in ann iad féin a fheiscint
id' spiorad soilseach,
claochlaithe mar a bheadh i sruthán gléineach
is grá acu duit as ucht gach nach iad.
Is mó de loinnir ná d'íomhá atá ionat
i m'aignese
Feicim i ngathanna thú
mílítheach mar sholas réaltaí ar bhalla liath
gearrshaolach mar scáil na heala báine
ag crithlonrú in uisce briste

Mither

Yer luve wis lik muinlicht
birlin sair theengs tae bonnieness,
So thit peerie thrawn sowls
Refleckin ilk ither agley
As in a creckit keekin gless…
Behauden in yer sheenin spreit
Thair ain refleckshun,
Chynged as in sheenin watter,
An luved ye fir whit they are not.
Yer less an eemage i ma mynd
Than a glowe
Ah glisk ye in leams
Whitely as sternlicht on a gray wa…
Mizzlin lik the refleckshun o a fite swan
Skimmerin on brucken watter.

The Tidings (Easter 1916)

Censored lies that mimic truth…
    Censored truth as pale as fear…
My heart is like a rousing bell —
    And but the dead to hear…

My heart is like a mother bird,
    Circling ever higher,
And the nest-tree rimmed about
    By a forest fire…

My heart is like a lover foiled
    By a broken stair —
They are fighting to-night in Sackville Street,
    And I am not there!

Scéala ó Éirinn (1916)

Bréaga na cinsireachta in áit na fírinne…
   An fhírinne chamtha, mílítheach mar sceimhle…
Mo chroíse ag preabadh mar chlog garg dúiseachta
   Na mairbh amháin atá ag éisteacht.

Mo chroíse mar mháthair-éan atá
   Ag guairdeall léi thuas, níos airde,
Crann na nide is é i mbaol
   Ag dóiteán foraoise.

Mo chroíse mar leannán atá
   Roimh staighre guagach—
Tá coimhlint anocht i Sráid Sackville
   Is nílimse ann chun buille a bhualadh!

The Tidings (Easter 1916)

Cast aboot lees thit eemitate truith…
Cast aboot truith as gash as dree…
Ma hert's lik a rowstin skillet…
An bit the deid tae hearken…

Ma hert's lik a mither burd,
Sweilin heicher an heicher,
An the nest-tree ringit roon aboot
Wi a forest lowe…

Ma hert is lik a luver lummed
Bi a brucken stair—
Thair fechtin the nicht in Sackville Street
An a'm no thair!

Iarfhocal/Afterword

2023 marks the 150th anniversary of the birth of Lola Ridge, in Dolphin's Barn, Dublin. It *should* have marked it.

By and large, it didn't. 150 years later she is still an unknown in Ireland, even among many of the poetry cognoscenti. Her Anarcho-Communist leanings prevented her popularity in the land of her birth; but we've grown up a little since, no?

The Poetry Foundation introduces her work as follows:

> Ridge was a poet and champion of the working class. Politically active before socialism became fashionable among New York intellectuals, Ridge participated in protests, marches, and pickets with ferocious spirit. Her writing is vigorous and electric. She was, as Peter Quartermain described her, "the nearest prototype in her time of the proletarian poet of class conflict, voicing social protest or revolutionary idealism".

And most of us have never heard of her! There's an uncompromising spirit at work in Ridge's poetry, a beautiful defiance of social and poetic convention. She is both *of* the people and *cut off* from the people: *of* the people in the sense of her compassionate identification with the newly arrived in New York, many of them Jewish, "snarling a weird Yiddish" in Henry James's shameful phrase.

By the time of her arrival in the Big Apple, about 30% of the city was Jewish, mostly from Russia and Eastern Europe. *Cut off*, not just from all the Henry Jameses of this world – she felt no loss there – but attracted and repulsed, equally, by the spreading sprawl.

To the American People
Will you feast with me, American People?
But what have I that shall seem good to you!
On my board are bitter apples
And honey served on thorns,
And in my flagons fluid iron,
Hot from the crucibles.

How should such fare entice you!

Do Mhuintir Mheiriceá

An suífdh sibh chun séire liom, a Mhuintir Mheiriceá?
Ach cad a bheadh agamsa a shásódh sibh?
Úlla searbha atá ar mo bhordsa
Mil á dáileadh agam agus dealga tríthi,
I mo chuidse flagún lacht d'iarann,
Te ón mbreogán.

Conas a mheallfadh lón mar sin sibh!

What put the iron in her veins? No doubt it was the revolutionary spirit of many of the immigrants with whom she associated in New York, enabling her to write a paeon to one of the greatest of them all, Emma Goldman, whose fearless writings and actions Lola would never have encountered had she remained in Ireland, or Australia. Her Scottish partner in America, David Lawson, was supportive of her work and ideals and they explored America together.

She worked wherever work could be found, in a factory, as an artist's model and as an illustrator – something of a Luftmensch at times – and found favour with many literary luminaries, for a while at least.

Not all poets lead admirable lives and Lola Ridge had feet of clay, no doubt. But just look at the way she observes those Jewish push-cart peddlers in New York. There's a saying, when life gives you lemons, sell them on the Lower East Side. Witness the empathetic vividness here:

> They are covering up the pushcarts…
> Now all have gone save an old man with mirrors—
> Little oval mirrors like tiny pools.
> He shuffles up a darkened street
> And the moon burnishes his mirrors till they shine like
>   phosphorus…
> The moon like a skull,
> Staring out of eyeless sockets at the old men trundling home
>   the pushcarts.

Brilliant! Deserving of a Pushcart Prize! The distinguished poet and anthologist, Louis Untermeyer, of German-Jewish background, writing of her poetry collection *The Ghetto*, wrote: "*The Ghetto* is essentially a book of the city, of its sodden brutalities, its sudden beauties."

She has been described by Professor Nancy Berke as the flaneuse of the urban spectacle. And what a spectacle that was, as she roamed the most densely populated area of all America. Imagine the sights, the sounds, the odours, the languages, infants sucking at the air, as she says – and the women:

> Their heads are uncovered to the stars,
> And they call to the young men and to one another
> With a free camaraderie
> Only their eyes are ancient and alone…

Our intentions here were simply to mark the 150th anniversary and to launch this modest trilingual chapbook in the month of her birth in the Eblana Club, Dún Laoghaire, Co. Dublin. We have not attempted to sum up her life and times – or her work – simply to whet the appetite of readers who may wish to explore her in more depth:

> "The frailest of humans physically and the poorest financially," was how avant-garde poet and litterateur Alfred Kreymborg described her, adding, "the woman on the spiritual barricade fighting with her pen against tyranny!"

Another vivid description of her:

> "One tall, thin figure of a woman stepped out alone, a good distance into the empty square, and when the police came down at her and the horse's hoofs beat over her head, she did not move, but stood with her shoulders slightly bowed, entirely still. The charge was repeated again and again, but she was not to be driven away…"
>
> (Katherine Anne Porter describing Lola Ridge's protest at the barbaric execution by electric chair of Sacco and Vanzetti).

"Radical, modernist, glamorous, feminist – adjectives and categories can only gesture toward the enduringly significant life and works of the poet Lola Ridge," writes Robert Pinsky, endorsing *Anything That Burns You: A Portrait of Lola Ridge, Radical Poet* by Terese Svoboda (Schaffner Press, 2018). Svoboda's book should be your first port of call if you wish to learn more about Lola as poet and activist.

For those who believe that political activism and poetry don't go together, the rousing poem below might serve as a wake-up call!

Reveille
Come forth, you workers!
Let the fires go cold—
Let the iron spill out, out of the troughs—
Let the iron run wild
Like a red bramble on the floors—
Leave the mill and the foundry and the mine
And the shrapnel lying on the wharves—
Leave the desk and the shuttle and the loom—
Come,
With your ashen lives,
Your lives like dust in your hands.
I call upon you, workers.
It is not yet light
But I beat upon your doors.
You say you await the Dawn
But I say you are the Dawn.
Come, in your irresistible unspent force
And make new light upon the mountains.
You have turned deaf ears to others—
Me you shall hear.
Out of the mouths of turbines,
Out of the turgid throats of engines,

Over the whistling steam,
You shall hear me shrilly piping.
Your mills I shall enter like the wind,
And blow upon your hearts,
Kindling the slow fire.
They think they have tamed you, workers—
Beaten you to a tool
To scoop up a hot honor
Till it be cool—
But out of the passion of the red frontiers
A great flower trembles and burns and glows
And each of its petals is a people.
Come forth, you workers—
Clinging to your stable
And your wisp of warm straw—
Let the fires grow cold,
Let the iron spill out of the troughs,
Let the iron run wild
Like a red bramble on the floors…
As our forefathers stood on the prairies
So let us stand in a ring,
Let us tear up their prisons like grass
And beat them to barricades—
Let us meet the fire of their guns
With a greater fire,
Till the birds shall fly to the mountains
For one safe bough.

Céadghairm

Amach libh, a oibrithe!
Ligigí do na tinte fuarú—
Ligigí don iarann doirteadh amach, amach as na humair—
Ligigí don iarann imeacht fiáin
Mar dhris dhearg ar na hurláir—
Fágaigí an muileann agus an teilgcheárta agus an mianach
Agus an srapnal ina luí ar na céanna—
Fágaigí an deasc agus an spól agus an seol—
Tagaigí,
Le bhur mbeatha mhílítheach,
An saol agaibh mar dhusta in bhur lámha.

Glaoimse oraibh, a oibrithe.
Níl ina lá fós
Ach táimse ag bualadh ar bhur ndoirse.
Deir sibh gur ag feithemh leis an gCamhaoir atá sibh
Ach deirimse libh gur sibhse an Chamhaoir.
Tagaigí le bhur bhfórsa dosháraithe neamhspíonta
Agus cruthaígí léas nua ar na sléibhte.

Cluas bhodhar a thug sibh do dhaoine eile—
Cloisfidh sibh mise, ámh.
As béal tuirbíní,
As scornach ata na n-inneall,
Os cionn na gaile is í ag feadaíl,
Cloisfidh sibh mé ag píobaireacht go géar.
Scuabfadsa isteach sna muilte agaibh im' ghaoth,
Is séidfead ar bhur gcroí,
Tine mhall agam á fadú.

Is dóigh leo go bhfuil sibh ceansaithe acu, a oibrithe
Buailte ina uirlis
Chun onóir the a ardú
Go dtí go bhfuaródh sí—
Ach as paisean na dteorainneacha dearga
Tá bláth mór ar crith, á dhó, lonraíonn sé
Agus pobal is ea gach peiteal de.

Amach libh, a oibrithe—
Agus greim agaibh ar bhur stábla
Agus ar bhur sop teolaí—
Ligigí do na tinte fuarú,
Ligigí don iarann doirteadh amach as na humair,
Ligigí don iarann imeacht fiáin
Mar dhris dhearg ar na hurláir…

Faoi mar do sheas ár sinsear ar na féarthailte
Seasaimisne i bhfáinne,
Stróicimis a gcuid príosún mar a stróicfí féar
Agus iad a bhascadh ina mbaracáidí—
In aghaidh thine a ngunnaí
Bíodh tine níos mó againne,
Go dtí go dteithfidh na héin chun na sléibhte
Chun tuirlingt ar chraobhóg shábháilte amháin.

I love the way that bird flies off to the mountain! There's a great spiritual breath of Whitmanesque freedom in the poetry of Lola Ridge which makes nonsense of the criticism that she was politically doctrinaire to the point of sacrificing the subtleties of poetry. She is a poet to her fingertips, sometimes more gritty than polished; she could master the long poem as much as the short and yet, in the Modernist spirit, always have something to say:

Babel
Oh, God did cunningly, there at Babel—
Not mere tongues dividing, but soul from soul,
So that never again should men be able
To fashion one infinite, towering whole.

Báibil
Ó, nár chliste é Dia ag Báibil
Teangacha agus anamacha óna chéile a scarúint,
Chun nach mbeadh daoine ábalta
Aon túr amháin infinideach a chruthú.

The Star
Last night
I watched a star fall like a great pearl into the sea,
Till my ego expanding encompassed sea and star,
Containing both as in a trembling cup.

An Réalt
Aréir
Bhreathnaíos ar réalta a thit mar mhórphéarla sa mhuir
Gur mhéadaigh ar an bhféin is gur chuimsigh muir is réalt
Iad araon mar a bheadh i gcorn ar crith.

It would seem that the impulse towards Anarchism contains within it dimensions that are beyond the socio-political realms. That is to say, true freedom not only takes away the shackles of statism, hierarchies, bureaucracy and authoritarianism from people, it aspires towards the limitlessness of the birthless, deathless self – the goal of all spiritual pursuit, which poetry often hints at – self-knowledge and cosmic consciousness:

Interim

The earth is motionless
And poised in space…
A great bird resting in its flight
Between the alleys of the stars.
It is the wind's hour off…

The wind has nestled down among the corn…
The two speak privately together,
Awaiting the whirr of wings.

Idirlinn

Tá an domhan gan chorraí
Agus crochta sa spás…
Éan ollmhór ag glacadh scíthe san eitilt dó
Idir lánaí na réalt.
Tá uair an chloig saor ag an ngaoth
Is í á soipriú féin san arbhar…
Iad i gcomhrá príobháideach lena chéile,
Ag feitheamh le seordán na sciathán.

The opening line of her poem *The Destroyer*, 'I am of the wind…' reminds this reader of an ancient druidic Irish poem, '*am gaeth ar muir*,' I am the wind on the sea.' Both poems, across centuries, echo the power of poetry and its place in the world. Wishful thinking? No, Lola Ridge was influential in her day. She made headlines when she and fellow poet Edna St Vincent Millay protested against the infamous execution of Sacco and Vanzetti, facing down the mounted police, as described earlier above. She championed several political prisoners such as unjustly incarcerated labour leader, Tom Mooney, son of Irish immigrants. Lola also worked in the educational sphere, ensuring that children would avail of progressive ideas.

1908, the year of Lola Ridge's arrival in New York. The scene depicted: two o'clock in the morning, near Brooklyn Bridge, N.Y., young news vendors, readying themselves for action.

Photo: Lewis Hine (National Child Labor Committee Collection, USA)

To top it all, she could also write with the insight of a child as in this extract from *Betty*:

> If you keep very still
> lizards will think you a stone
> and run over your lap
> Butterflies' liveries
> are scarlet and black.
> They drive chariots in air.
>   People in the chariots
> are pale as dew—
> you can see right through them—
> but the chariots
> are made of gold of the sun.
> They go up to heaven
> and never catch fire…

Lots of factors are said to have contributed to the sudden decline of her reputation, not least the rise of McCarthyism in the US, her loss of patronage and problems with curatorship.

One can only hope that the 150th anniversary might generate new interest in her work, particularly in the land of her birth. A plaque? A statue, perhaps, a mural or some such monument? A prize in her name? The Lola Ridge International Prize for Socially Engaged Poetry.

A Chríoch/End
A note on John McDonald and Gabriel Rosenstock

John McDonald is a haiku master who writes in Scots. Gabriel Rosenstock is a poet, tankaist, haikuist, novelist, playwright, children's author and translator. He transcreated haiku by John McDonald in the book *Tea wi the Abbot* (The Onslaught Press 2016), described by Alan Titley, Professor Emeritus of Modern Irish, UCC, as "an invitation to see more clearly, to hear more sharply, to feel more soulfully. If we have at all those eyes to see and those ears to hear they wake us up, not only to taste the language, but to hear the music of wonder. These verbal explosions echo in the chambers of wisdom".

www.ingramcontent.com/pod-product-compliance
Lightning Source LLC
Chambersburg PA
CBHW042122100526
44587CB00025B/4156